The
Science of
Gravity

John Stringer

RSVP
RAINTREE
STECK-VAUGHN
P U B L I S H E R S
A Steck-Vaughn Company

Austin, Texas

www.steck-vaughn.com

Science World

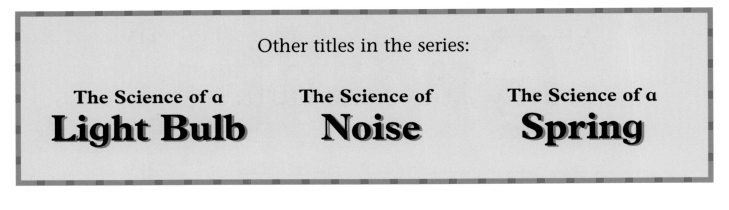

Other titles in the series:

The Science of a
Light Bulb

The Science of
Noise

The Science of a
Spring

Picture acknowledgments
The publishers would like to thank the following for allowing their pictures to be reproduced in this book: Eye Ubiquitous 12, /Adina Tovy Amsel 16 (bottom)/A.J.G. Bell 14, /NASA *cover* (main), 10, 18; Genesis 4; Getty Images/Ken Fisher *title page*, 24, /Dan Ham *cover* (inset top), /Chris Noble 15, /Mark Wagner 7, /Tim Young 8; Angela Hampton *cover* (inset middle), 6 (top); Science Photo Library/John Bavesi 16 (top), /NASA 17, 19 (both), /Novosti 21, /David Nunuk 22, /Bill Sanderson 6 (bottom), /Kaj R. Svensson *contents page*, 20, /Jerry Wachter 23; Wayland Picture Library 5 (all), 9, 11. **Illustrator:** Peter Bull

Published by Raintree Steck-Vaughn Publishers, an imprint of Steck-Vaughn Company

Printed in Italy. Bound in the United States.
1 2 3 4 5 6 7 8 9 0 04 03 02 01 00

Library of Congress Cataloging-in-Publication Data
Stringer, John.
The science of gravity / John Stringer.
        p.   cm.—(Science world)
Includes bibliographical references and index.
Summary: Introduces the force of gravity and discusses its effects and reasons for variations in its strength.
ISBN 0-7398-1323-4
1. Gravitation—Juvenile literature.
2. Gravity—Juvenile literature.
[1. Gravity.]
I. Title. II. Series.
QC178.S88   2000
531'.14—dc21   99-16529

Contents

What Is Gravity?

Gravity is an invisible force that pulls together any two objects. It pulls us down toward our planet, Earth, and holds us there. We can't see it, but we can see its effects.

Why don't we always feel the pulling force of gravity? Usually, the force is too weak to feel. But it gets stronger the more mass something has. So what's big and heavy and very close to you? It's the planet we live on, Earth. That's why you can feel the pull between you and Earth.

▼ Only Earth is huge enough to have a force of gravity we can feel.

The strength of gravity's pull

How strong is the pull of gravity on the objects in these pictures? Is it weak? Or is it strong? (Clue: look at the mass of the objects.)

◀ There is a strong pull of gravity between the bulls and the ground.

There is a strong pull of ▶ gravity between the castle and the ground.

▼ The pull of gravity between these two people is weak.

▼ The pull of gravity between the flower and the butterfly is weak.

Falling

Have you ever wondered why something falls down when you drop it, and not sideways or up? Objects fall down because of the force of gravity. It pulls them toward the center of the earth.

When you throw a ball into the air, ▶ the force of gravity pulls it toward the ground.

Sir Isaac Newton and gravity

Sir Isaac Newton was a famous scientist who lived about 300 years ago. One story says that he saw an apple fall from a tree, and it started him thinking. "Why does everything fall downward? It's as if there is a force pulling everything toward the center of the earth." The pulling force he thought about is called gravity. He thought that everything that had mass was attracted to everything else.

Any two objects have a force of gravity between them. Everything around you is affected by gravity. Objects that are huge have more gravity between them than objects with less mass. The earth is so huge that it pulls everything downward. That is just as well. Without gravity you would float off into space.

Some ferries are huge. ▶ They are not nearly as large as the earth. But when two ferries are docked next to each other, they are pulled together. There is a force of gravity between them.

Moving objects without touching them

There are other invisible forces like gravity. Magnetism is an invisible force. Magnets can pull objects without touching them. Magnets pull objects made of iron and steel and some other metals.

Sometimes magnets can pull other magnets toward them. Sometimes they can push other magnets away from them.

▼ The force of magnetism has pulled these metal paper clips on to a magnet.

Magnets can work through other materials. You can move paper clips around with a magnet under the table. A strong magnet will even pull through your hand. It can also work through water.

How does gravity compare with magnetism?

Force	Can it pull objects together?	Can it push objects apart?	Is it invisible?	Will it work with any two objects?
Gravity	Yes	No	Yes	Yes
Magnetism	Yes	Yes	Yes	No

In some ways gravity is like magnetism. It is also invisible and it works without touching. If you are flying in an airplane, gravity is still pulling you down. If you are swimming in the sea, it does also.

◀ You can create a chain of paper clips. Hold a magnet above a pile of paper clips. You will notice that the paper clips move toward the magnet, drawn by its attraction. The magnetism travels through each paper clip attached to the magnet. Soon you will have a chain.

How Does Gravity Affect You?

You need muscles and bones to keep your body shape against the pull of gravity. Without gravity, you would have no weight, and you would float off into space.

▼ When in space, astronauts can float around. There is almost no gravity to give them weight.

Weight and mass

The pull of the earth is strong for two reasons. The earth is very, very heavy. It weighs about 6.5 sextillion tons, and you are standing on it. The earth's gravity is pulling down on you all the time. We call that pull your weight.

Collapsing men from Mars!

The science-fiction writer H. G. Wells wrote a famous book about an invasion of Earth by Martians, called *The War of the Worlds*. In it, the Martians had to build themselves machines for walking around. Because gravity is much less on Mars, their bodies weren't strong enough for Earth's gravity!

When you hold a ball, you can feel the ▶ weight of it in your hand. This is because gravity pulls the ball into your hands, giving it weight.

Losing weight but not mass!

You have weight because of the pull between you and the earth. The mass is what you are made from. Your mass stays the same, wherever you are. But if you go to the moon or a planet, your weight can change.

▼ This astronaut has almost no weight while he is floating around in space. But his body, his mass, remains the same.

Does your weight change on the moon?

Earth has about six times more mass than our moon. When astronauts went there, their mass stayed the same. But the pull between them and the moon was about six times less than the pull between them and Earth. Their weight on the moon was one-sixth of their weight on Earth. For this reason, they could leap around like grasshoppers!

If you go to another planet, the pull of gravity will change. If the planet is bigger and heavier than Earth, the pull will be stronger. If the planet is smaller than Earth, the pull will be weaker.

Gravity is like a bungee jump in ▶ reverse. When you leave Earth, gravity pulls you back. (Unlike a bungee cord, though, it doesn't pull harder the farther you go.)

On a tiny planet, the pull of ▶ gravity is so small that you could easily jump very high.

On a huge planet, the ▶ pull of gravity would drag you down. You would feel heavy and find it hard to jump.

Lighter up a mountain

You have weight because of the pull between your mass and the earth's mass. Your mass stays the same, wherever you are. However, your weight can change. It changes if you get farther away from the center of the earth.

▼ The nearer you are to the center of the earth, the more you weigh. At the bottom of a valley, you weigh a little more than you weigh on a mountaintop!

▼ The farther you are from the center of the earth, the less you weigh. Climb to the top of a mountain, and you lose weight—but not mass. The bathroom scales will still give you the same reading when you come down.

Weightlessness

Have you ever been over a curved bridge in a car? Have you ever been on a fast, bumpy carnival ride? For a moment, you might have felt as if you had no weight. This is how you would feel if there were no gravity on our planet. Gravity gives you weight and keeps you on the ground.

▼ You feel weightless on a Ferris wheel when you're spun around the top, traveling back down to the bottom.

Your backbone is ▶ made up of large bones called vertebrae. They are held apart by soft disks. On Earth, gravity presses on the soft disks. When you are weightless, the disks are not pressed as much. You actually become almost three quarters of an inch (2 cm) taller!

If you go far enough into space, you can be very far from any planets or stars. Then their gravity hardly acts on you. You become almost weightless. Your body will still have the same mass. But because there is almost no pull of gravity, you will float around with no up or down.

▼ In a space shuttle, one astronaut can float upside down, while another astronaut is upright!

Living in space

Astronauts who have been weightless for some time notice some strange changes to their bodies. The blood inside the body gets pumped by the heart all over the body. When weightless, astronauts' blood is still being pumped "up" to their heads. There is no gravity to pull the blood back down, so their faces swell. Also, they aren't using their legs to hold their bodies up. Their muscles and bones soon get weaker. After some time in the new conditions, their bodies adjust.

▲ The heart of an astronaut beats ten times a minute slower after being weightless for a while.

This astronaut is chasing a weightless ▶ sandwich around his living area.

While in space, every object floats that isn't anchored. Astronauts have to be careful when they move around their living area. Objects still have the same mass, and large objects could hurt them if they run into them.

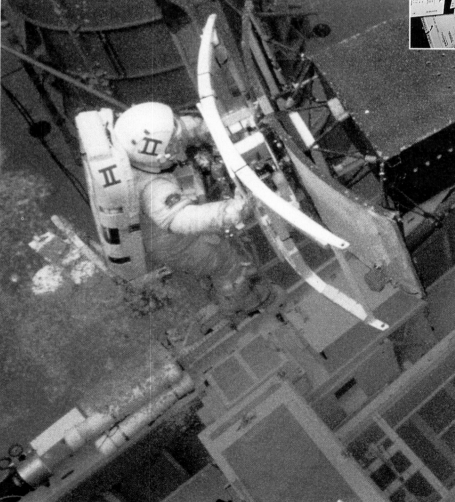

◀ Astronauts train underwater to create weightless effects similar to those in space. This helps them learn how to move in weightless conditions.

Other strong forces

Sometimes you feel strong forces, such as when you are on an amusement park ride. When you go around a sharp corner in a car, also, your body keeps moving in one direction. The car or ride suddenly moves in a different direction. This can make you feel dizzy or even sick.

▼ Amusement park rides like this one go upside down. They swing from side to side at a fast speed. You can feel strong forces acting on you.

Your ear is the organ that senses the pull of gravity. It has fluid-filled spaces called semicircular canals. The fluid moves about as you move and bends tiny hairs. This tells the brain what direction you're leaning toward and whether you're upright. If you are weightless, or when you are pressed by very strong forces, you may feel sick. Sometimes the brain can't make sense of the messages.

How do you get used to strong forces?

Pilots and astronauts are trained to become used to strong forces. They may ride on the end of a huge machine that spins them faster and faster. They feel a force several times the force of their own weight.

Center of gravity

Every object has its mass and weight centered on one point. This imaginary point is called the center of gravity. Exactly where the center of gravity is depends on the object's shape. A tall object with most of its mass at the top has a high center of gravity. A short object with its mass centered at the base has a low center of gravity.

◀ Objects with a high center of gravity are more likely to fall over than objects with a low center of gravity. Tall vehicles, such as trucks, have their heavy parts, the engine and axles, as low as possible. This creates a low center of gravity. This truck would have to lean a long way before it fell over. Its center of gravity is close to the ground.

If you could drill a hole through the center of the earth, you would come out the other side. You would drill right through the earth's center of gravity.

▲ This gymnast is constantly changing her position as she moves. She balances more easily when her center of gravity is low down—close to the bar. When she stands on her feet, her center of gravity is high up and she finds balancing harder. When she does a handstand, her center of gravity is higher up and it is even harder for her to keep her balance.

If you dropped a ball down the hole, it would travel back and forth through the hole. Finally it would come to rest in the very middle—Earth's center of gravity.

Gravity Above the Earth's Surface

Gravity still pulls on objects when they aren't on the earth's surface. Everything above you—airplanes, birds, and even the moon—is moved by gravity's pull. In fact, everything in the air above the earth is falling. But most objects use speed and air resistance to fly and land safely.

These people are jumping ▶ out of an airplane high above the ground. Each person has a parachute in a bag on his or her back. Pulling a string releases the parachute from the bag. It allows the people to fall safely to the ground.

Friction of air moving across the parachute, inside and outside, helps slow down the fall.

Air slows you down in two ways. First, the parachute fills with air, and the air pushes up on the parachute. Second, the air slips over the surface of the parachute. And the drag of it holds you back. This is called air resistance.

The trapped air escapes through a small central hole. This keeps the parachute from swinging and "spilling" out the air, making the parachutist feel sick.

The parachutist is pulled toward the center of the earth by the force of gravity.

Staying up

Stand by for takeoff. Stand by for the great tug of war. On the down team—gravity! On the up team—the lift from the airplane. But how will we give the airplane lift? Of course! Engines to full throttle, or speed. If enough air flows over the wings, fast enough, the airplane will go up.

▲ We're rushing forward. Air is streaming over the wings. Because of their special shape, they're giving us lift. Gravity is losing. The airplane is climbing.

How do gliders stay in the air?

Gliders can stay in the air for a long time without an engine. Gliders use their long wings to soar up on thermals. These are huge columns of rising air. Without the thermals, gravity would pull the glider down.

▲ Whoops! We're out of fuel. The airplane is slowing down. The air over the wings is slowing down, too. We haven't enough lift. Gravity is winning! Stand by for a crash landing!

27

Gravity's pull on the planets

The planets in our solar system are moving around the sun. They are kept in orbit by gravity. Some of the planets have moons orbiting around them. Others have rings. All these are held in space by the forces of gravity.

▼ This picture shows the sun and the planets in our solar system. You can see the thick rings around Saturn.

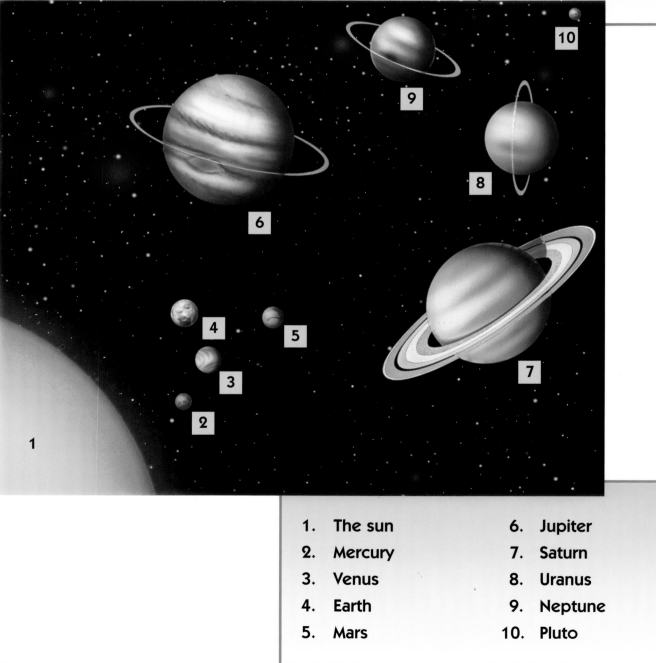

1.	The sun	6.	Jupiter
2.	Mercury	7.	Saturn
3.	Venus	8.	Uranus
4.	Earth	9.	Neptune
5.	Mars	10.	Pluto

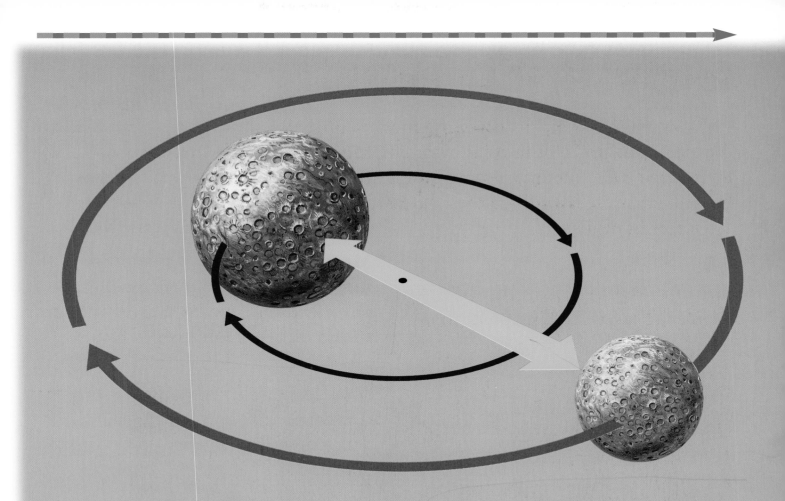

▲ Pluto (left) and Charon (right) in orbit. They both orbit the same point. It's as if the two planets are holding hands and swinging around in a circle.

The earth's moon orbits the earth's center of gravity. The planet Pluto has such a huge moon, Charon, that Pluto and Charon have nearly the same mass. As they both nearly equal the same mass, they both orbit a point in space between them. They are like a pair of dancers holding hands.

What are black holes?

A black hole is caused by a very dense, heavy object that has a huge gravitational pull. This acts like a space funnel. Anything pulled into the space funnel can never escape.

escape. Maybe it's not what some people think

Glossary

Air resistance The slowing down force of air on moving objects.

Astronauts Members of a crew on a spacecraft.

Center of gravity The point in an object where its weight is evenly balanced.

Force A push or a pull between objects.

Gravity The force of attraction between two objects. The greater their mass, and the closer they are, the greater the force of gravity between them.

Gravitational Having something to do with gravity.

Magnetic field The area around a magnet where the magnetic effect can be detected.

Magnetism The invisible force of a magnet. It is strongest at the ends, or poles, of a magnet.

Mass The amount of matter in something. The mass of something never changes. Its weight will change with a different force of gravity.

Muscles Strong body tissues that can get shorter and longer. These actions allow us to move parts of the body.

Resistance Something that tends to stop movement. Air resistance is the slowing-down force of air.

Weight The force exerted on an object by the earth. An object's weight depends on its mass.

Weightlessness When you are in space, far from the gravitational pull of the stars and planets, you are almost weightless.

Further Information

Books to read

Hatchett, Clint. *Space Travel* (Outer Space). Danbury, CT: Grolier, 1998.

Hewitt, Sally. *Forces Around Us* (It's Science). Danbury, CT: Children's Press, 1998.

Oxlade, Chris. *Science Magic with Magnets* (Science Magic). Hauppauge, NY: Barron's, 1995.

Oxlade, Chris, and Martin Hollins. *Forces* (A BBC Fact Finders Book). Jersey City, NJ: Parkwest, 1996.

Riley, Peter. *Our Solar System*. Westport, CT: Joshua Morris, 1998.

Snedden, Robert. *Forces*. Des Plaines, IL: Heinemann, 1999.

White, Larry. Gravity: *Simple Experiments for Young Scientists* (Gateway Science). Brookfield, CT: Millbrook Press, 1995.

Web sites to visit

http://ericir.syr.edu/Projects/Newton/newtonalpha This site contains many interesting science lessons.

www.lsc.org
This is the home page of the Liberty Science Center

www.discoveryplace.org
This is the home page of Discovery Place

Places to visit

Liberty Science Center, Liberty State Park, Phillip Street, Jersey City, NJ (Tel: 201-200-1000). This outstanding science museum has hands-on activities guided by the museum staff.

Discovery Place, 301 North Tryon Street, Charlotte, NC (Tel: 1-800-935-0553). This is an award-winning science and technology museum featuring hands-on experiments.

Index

Numbers in **bold** refer to pictures as well as text.